Openings 38

The Poetry Society of the Open University

Annual Anthology

of

OU Poets

2021

Published 2021 by Open University Poets.

ISBN 978-0-9567833-9-4

Editor: Sue Spiers
Cover: Folies, Bergère poster Maurice Biris

Printed by Lulu.com

Lulu

Introduction

OU Poets is the Poetry Society of the Open University. It is open to any student or staff member, past or present. At the time of going to press there are about 80 members from all over the U.K. with some in mainland Europe and worldwide.

Members of the society submit poems to a magazine, which is produced 5 times a year, each one having a different voluntary editor. The magazine is not a publication *per se* and is strictly produced by the members for the members. There is a section for comment and criticism of members' work.

At the end of the year, members are asked to vote for the 20 poems they most appreciated from the 5 magazines produced that year. Those with the most votes, allowing for no more than one poem per poet, appear in the following year's issue of Openings. The anthology is as broad-based as the society itself and reflects the varied backgrounds, interests and tastes of the members.

If you would like more information about OU Poets, please contact the Secretary:

Kimberley Pulling
secretary@oupoets.org.uk

or the Chair:

Polly Stretton
chair@oupoets.org.uk
Tel: (+44) 1886 830054 for postal address information.

Or visit our website at http://www.oupoets.org.uk

@OUPoets

Contents

Contents

Cate Cody

The Earth said *Listen*

I rake my feet through leaves,
loud like crisps teased
from packets
then I stop

I stop to hear the earth
absorb the fog,
sparkling and
expanding, like milk poured on
childhood cornflakes

then I listen to the breeze
squeezing her way through my hair
and skin and I welcome her in,
lungs breathing deeply

the Earth said *listen*
I hear her,
I marvel, she glistens

Jenny Hamlett

Mother

You come at me
carrying the flame of your anger
like an Olympic torch

I'm transfixed

can't say what I feel
don't know what I think.

You were always off the cuff
with your speech, flaring up;
dying away to grey ash and yet …

these words, *You've ruined my life,*
are musket shots.

I wish I'd fought back
I was numb
before your avenging angel.

It wasn't until you died
I understood.
I was not your kind of woman

and yet, when you woke from a coma
saying, *Jenny*, pleased that I was there
then I knew …

between us lay, if not liking,
at least love.

Barbara Cumbers

This is a house in Northwood

This is the woman
who lives in a house in Northwood

This is the cat who sits on the knees
of the well-off woman with a life of ease
who wants to do good if the cat agrees
who lives in a house in Northwood

This is the news that's watched on TV
by the privileged woman with a cat on her knee
who would like to do good but doesn't know how
who only reacts to a loud miaow
and who lives in a house in Northwood.

These are the people too starving to stand
of the wrong religion in a far-off land
who are seen on the news through do-nothing eyes
along with the sport and the bake-off prize
by the good Christian woman who cuddles her cat
who she noticed today is getting fat
in a warm, dry house in Northwood.

These are the bombs that are made over here
sold to any who'll pay for reasons unclear,
that are dropped on the people too starving to stand
who want peace to come to their ruined land
who are seen on the news through privileged eyes
along with the thrillers and stories of spies
by the well-meaning woman who's busy right now

but who'd like to do good if she only knew how
who gives her cat the best of food
who's proud of suburban rectitude
and who lives in a house in Northwood.

Rob Lowe

Star-child

Excited by the night
And by her place in it,
She puts up her soft hood,
Crosses the rye-grass lawn.

Wild creature in a wood,
Pink daisies round her feet,
She opens a latched gate,
Quiet as a stalking cat.

She pads on softened ground:
Embedded in its crust
Part of earth and earthy,
She belongs to the flesh.

Yet her cheeks are smooth air,
Her hair is cirrus white;
Wide eyes make floating moons,
Her thoughts glitter like stars.

The universe is hers
And she belongs to it:
Escaped from whom she is,
Her steps become the whole.

Sally Charnock

Sayings

He said
I don't like you
She said why
He said
Your ambitions
Are far too high
And she replied
I'm here to do, not to try.

Kimberley Pulling

A Postcard from November

Off-white against the sheets. How many thumbs
have held it, turned it over, tossed it back
unsent upon the desk. What could they write?

Wish you were here – amongst these off-white walls,
parked cars, pub tables, under a weak sky
where Torbay palms pretend exotic climes?

The hotel's nice – the 1970s called,
they want their rest home back. Too hot, and tired.
Paintings of fat pink women grace the walls.

Great view – outside my window, there's that 'palm'
uplit by halogen security lights,
and then the road. Beyond, I guess, the sea.

Food's good – if bent-fork breakfasts are your thing,
warm trays of rubber eggs – and there's a bar
(to get a drink, you have to ring the bell).

The weather's fine – a Dorset hurricane,
the Caribbean finally come to town.
The greyed nets billow where the glazing's blown.

I'm missing you already – No. I'm not.
Outside, the battered cordyline fights on;
her heavy flowerbags catch in the squall,
straining capriciously her slender bole;
her ragged petioles thrash in the swirling
current, like a drowning woman's hair.

Indentured to a life as something else,
what would she give for these three days away?
This anywhere, this time and space to think

about the southern rains, the sunny days,
the long white cloud, and how the Cook Strait wind
blows fierce across the unpolluted skies
where, only half a world away, it's Spring.

Kathy Finney

My Last Afternoon with Grandma A
for Harriet

Sat, moulded in a moulded chair
as the pip-pip-pip
of the monitor morphs with Nan's muttering.

Shrunk to the size of a sparrow
she nests, hands pecking
at perfect hospital corners, and chitters –

the doctor had to shave me locks
on account of t'scarlet fever, lass
tha'rt looks like thi mother to a tee
have a haupney fur cinder toffee,
father's fetched a ribbon from t' fair
sithee mother it's as red as me hair –

when I lift her onto the commode, hair shedding
like worn out feathers, heart fluttering
to be free of its bony cage.

14

Nigel Pearce

Again, for Sylvia Plath

I am in your repose rested in a speckled rose grave,
a tomb in a canopy of willows weeping,
your bejewelled soul is purple and enticing my fountain.
A pen weaves willow within it.

An entombed fragrance can be so sweetly stoned,
ablaze with your lights legal and purple,
my pen murmured and ejaculated on a page,
Poetry is the blood jet.
You said

Sue Spiers

Break-up

Having moved into her new home
she had to deal with the spider alone.
It; crouched and balled. Her; unblinking.

It seemed to still itself in fake demise.
She was not fooled, kept it in sight
in case it disappeared into a crevice

in her room, roaming at will overnight.
She took a jar from the bedroom shelf,
emptied out the make-up brushes,

gingerly upturned it over the spider.
She looked for something to trap it,
slid a meal-for-one cardboard sleeve

between the carpet and the creature.
The prison was right sided, the lid
punctured for air, and weighted down.

In the morning the spider was still there
having contentedly spun a home
and splayed in the glory of fresh web.

She put the jar and its contents
by her doorstep and binned the lid,
proud of herself at dealing humanely.

Days later the spider was still there,
desiccated and translucent in the web
spun in its panic trying to escape.

Peter Meredith-Smith

Motorway

Motorway
  straight-curved
    carves me home
      through rock and earth
        hawk observed
          hot-tar gone cold
            holds tyres' grip
          as fleeting fields
        whisk time away
      observed with
    mirrored eyes
  trees exploding green
crown fractured rock
  where cold theodolites
    marked the blasting spot
      there diesel-fuelled
        navvies cut and
          scarred this lady's side
           exposed her beauty
             to my intruders' eyes
              surveyed now with
                pistoned-speed
              the passing fields
            are disfigured by the
          concrete strut of
        M-whatever's
      calculated
    route to
  labour's
   end

Katherine Rawlings

Turn the Key Softly

In this house of many windows
and this house of many doors
where dust lies thick upon the shelves
and thick upon the floors,
I will wipe clear the leaden panes
and vacuum up the dust
so it is a home again for us.

When you turn the key, my love,
as softly as long past,
let us forget the tearful years
and smile with arms out-thrust.

This house locked up for painful years
will open once again
and as we hold each other's hands
our light renewed will glow
between us and illuminate
with ever binding love
our halls and corridors.

Peta-Maria Slaney

It's Not His Fault

He must love me, he says he does.
He will be kind, he promises so.
He's not controlling, he just wants the best for me.
He's taking care of me, it's for my own good.
He says I complete him, I never knew I had that power.
He doesn't pursue other girls, he's just looking.
He is traditional, I'll be so happy as a housewife.
I'm doing it wrong, he will show me a better way.
I don't look my best, he will recommend a new style.
Brown hair doesn't suit me, he thinks red would be better.
My friends are no good for me, he and I are a good team.
My family take me for granted, we don't need them.
I don't need a car, he will take me anywhere I need to go.
I am irrational and unreasonable, it's good he's so patient.
I am suspicious and paranoid, how could I think that of
                                    him?
It's not manipulation, he's just trying to help me.
It's not abuse, he's just showing how I make him feel.
It's my fault, I shouldn't have made him angry.
He doesn't like doing this, I've made him be the bad guy.
He will forgive me this time, but I must try harder.
It's not his fault.
I was asking for it.
I made him do it.
I'm impossible to live with.
No one else would want me.
I am unlovable.
I am ugly.
I am stupid.
I am difficult.

20

I should be grateful to have him.
He didn't mean to.
I made him do it.

Julie Stuart

The Day Alex Sank the Boat

The day Alex sank the boat
The sea was translucent grey green
while
early summer clouds slipped greased
into an adolescent sunrise.

Rocks along the cove
split the horizon with sharp taloned nails
and saltwater lapped laughing
as we tumbled
head over heels
into ice blue cold water.

The day Alex sank the boat
morning sea shimmered summer froth
while
cooler beer slid down unquenchable necks.
Midships
the boat lurched drunkenly
failing to find level
pitched to one side.

And drowned.

Lem Ibbotson

The Uses of Old Age

When you are old, what is there left?
Of many things now, you find you're bereft:
Eyesight is fading, vigour is gone,
Passion is spent, though affection lives on.
You walk with a stick and are generally told,
You look old.

If you've bypassed the popular singers' yells
And avoided the damaging decibels
Your hearing survives, and good music is there
To enjoy at your ease in your easy chair.
You're just old fashioned, you're told,
But you're old.

Then there's the love of poetry
Something to write while you still can see
Traditional verse that rhymes
Though you've heard it so many times,
Such verse is outdated, you're told.
So okay: you're old!

Polly Stretton

The Skin of the Selkie
a simple retelling of the myth

Scottish tales told in the flickering flames of fire
tell of maidens dancing in the moonlight.
There are three with black hair, dark-shining eyes
and soft olive skin, watched by three brothers.

Pity the selkies, who love to dance in warmth
on the shore. At midnight they discard sealskins,
squeeze out from the balmy humidity,
cast off the sweaty ozone of the cold sea.

They're seaweed slippery – borne into the world,
prance free on the sands, arms stretched to the winds,
dance and twirl, sing to the sky, coves, caves, cliffs,
and three brothers watch them – for hours – hours.

The eldest says, *Collect the sealskins and say,*
'I have your selkie skin, I claim you for my bride.'
The first two call for their maids, then the youngest –
he's fallen for the selkie whose skin he won.

My love is greater than the world's oceans,
he cried, claims her, watches her simple yearning.
In his heart he sees the sorrows of the world
for she will always belong to the oceans.

The sealskins are secreted, locked away,
if the brides find them it's back to the water.
The young lad can't bear his selkie's pining,
he yields her sealskin, she returns to the sea.

The oldest lad's bride tracks down her sealskin.
But the middle boy burns his bride's seal pelt;
she rushes to save it and dies in the flames.
The flickering flames of the fire. He expires.

The youngest brother weeps on the seashore
praying his bride will return to his side.
She swims to the shoreline every ninth night,
cools on a conch shell, dances with him again.

Phil Craddock

Taking a Poem for a Walk

It yowls, it whimpers
it paces up and down
it doesn't let me concentrate
on things more important.

It whines, it stares at me
it hangs out its tongue.
Defeated, I put on
my jacket and shoes

and, keeping it firmly
held on a lead
I walk it out the front door
and into the street.

There, it pads along
lithely beside me
moving to the measure
of my steady stride

gradually forming
a rhythm of its own
a theme and a narrative
a metre and a style.

And then, through the gate
to the wide, green park
it tugs, it pulls
it strains to be free.

And once untethered
it sprints away, foot-sure
running and racing
leaping and jumping.

Ideas burst out
tumbling and turning
thought after thought
phrase after phrase

bounding, pouncing
snapping, grabbing,
spinning, twisting,
rolling, wrestling.

And that's when I take out
my notebook and pencil
and immortalise it all
on paper.

If only I'd remembered
my notebook and pencil.

It yaps at me all the way home.

Judi Moore

Goosey, goosey

On the wet grass in the orchard
lies a tiny goosedown feather.
Here they come, him and her. Takes me
straight back to St Keverne, that afternoon
when I was seven, we visited with
mother's cousin and their children.

We kids were playing in their farmyard,
then I saw I'd been abandoned.
Everyone was somewhere else, but here *they* came:
a honking gaggle, geese and gander
half-flying at me, cross the courtyard –
the Roman goose-guard in full cry:
none of them looked kindly upon strangers,
even small ones such as I.

Don't slip me your white feather, goosey,
I am bigger now, and braver.
I know more of how the world works.

And I have had your kind for dinner.

Hilary Mellon

PEACOCK

Bewildered by the blue of you
that lingering iridescence
that glimmer of you

that petrol sheen
sleek-as-a-plastic-raincoat
under-a-street-light blue

then that electric blue
which turns to turquoise
when the lights turn

flashing over and over you
fired from a disco ball
until I'm shot right through

with shards of emerald green
of splintered bronze
and then a sudden wash

that thin glaze of liquid silver
coating all those blues
which make up you.

Alice Harrison

How to Fall off the Wagon

Experience a setback –
     lose a job or a relationship or something.
Find a run-down backstreet pub –
     lino on the floor, a cold draught from
     the never-closed door, someone in the corner
     talking to himself.
Inhale the aroma of stale beer and failure.
Decide a half is neither here nor there.
Buy a half.

Move to a smarter pub –
     lunchtime, business men, shopping women.
Nurse a pint for some hours –
feel resentment growing, hide envy with scorn.
Eye the women like you've learnt not to.
Measure the men.

Realise it's evening –
     the atmosphere more congenial.
Buy another pint and perhaps a chaser.
Listen to conversations, appreciate witticisms –
     several men look like they've got things sussed,
     several women look like they're laughs.
Buy another drink, make a remark, join in general banter.
Buy another drink.
Offer drinks all round.
Enjoy a brief and truthful eloquence.
Start a sing-song.
Feel the warmth and camaraderie.
Lurch to the bar often through blaring and receding noise.

Perceive a slight –
    a comment made, a drink spilt.
Experience an overwhelming rush of grudges.
Act on them.
Resign to being manhandled outside.

Wake next morning –
    somehow at home in stained clothes.
Feel shame, déjà vu, relief –
    you by-passed the maudlin stage.
Decide against a fried breakfast, any breakfast.

Now put your head in your hands.

Julie Stamp

After

I will see you again, I will hug you again,
we will do all the things that we love.
I will be there again, you will come here again,
we've had sorrow and distance enough.
We will be close again, we will talk once again,
we will laugh and share plans like before:
let us feel safe again and look forward again
to the times we will share and much more.
Let us keep going on, let us keep well and strong,
let's believe that this isn't forever;
let us see the same moon, let us see the same sun,
let's feel blessed that we'll soon be together.

M. C. Gardner

The Rook

it filled the air
it was back
the rook
the tango dancer
a spectre of the night

blossom blacked all
the Moon was dead
disturbed by the wind
by reels of rain
it crushed the air

it hovered over the hill
sliding down, down…
its feathers whispered
brushed away – indecision?
then nothing at all –

Adrian Green

From *Estuary Haiku – An April Journal*

a kayak alone
skimming the estuary tide,
welcoming springtime

late geese ride the tide
head north for summer – winter's
eel-grass discarded

across the shingle
sanderlings flock to the edge –
waves break into spring

crowstone at sunset,
where the Thames turns into sea
the estuary breathes

a freighter swings at
anchor, wakes at the stirring
of wind from the east

east from the island,
boats creep along Hadleigh Ray,
anticipate sea

dunlins busy at
the margins, summer beckons
their passage elsewhere

pebbles roll under
waves, a beach sings through the spray,
grinds shells into sand

Ross McGivern

Heron

On baked ground of a blistered bank,
Heron nestles within parched reeds.
She eyes me from her angled elegance,
gauges if I am threat to nest or need.
Dipping her perfect head to neck a drink,
I pause as she catches her mirrored face.
Yellow eyes arch, as I slow to think
if she knows her potent solitary grace.
I crane further over bullrush to admire
the dazzling beauty of this lonesome bird,
whose dalliances break the water's smile
and awkward squawkish song is rarely heard.
Resplendent wings launch her East. I swallow,
wishing I took my chance to follow.

Ted Griffin

Such are Thoughts

A newspaper meandering on the cricket pitch:
Small boys chattering in trebled glee:
Great cheers on passing to the big school.

This childhood trying to dictate all my fate.

The last leaf on the Autumn tree falling while we sit:
Rotten apples exhausted on the lawn:
My first girlfriend, all blonde and bottom.

Youth and the basic appeal of sex.

The boss trying to understand the new age:
Hard winters with snow packing in before the car:
The damp, sleeping dog smells before the fire:

My young man days, and I know it all.

Later, that appears another time of love:
Hands sink deep into brown and scented hair:
True passion, heavy with uncontented moments.

My adulthood and true appreciation.

Over eighty and sinking into slumbers:
That old chair is gratefully received:
But, thankfully, this G and T still retains its flavour.

Old age with all the taxes paid; and what is left but art and
death?

Denis Ahern

First Visit

Like in any new experience
the wide-eyed kid is keen,
eagerly entering this hall
of boxes and trestle tables.

Kindly women smile,
they're a bit like Grandma,
and a man with a beard
does a nod and half-wink.

There's too much to see,
too many distractions
for the kid to notice the dread,
the worry in Mum's eyes.

She follows her toddling boy,
a yearling in her arms,
approaches the table,
offers a slip of paper.

To the kid the draped cloth
down the table front
is a place to hide, a game,
he likes it here.

A transaction takes place above.
Below in his secret cave
the kid knows no one will find him
until mum reaches for his hand
and they leave, ending
their first visit to a food bank.

Vicki Morley

The Hem of the Day

The hem of the day
is tucked into my nightdress
making sleep impossible
voices repeat   repeat
unravelling careful stiches
ends fray   threads   separate.

The garment mutates
spools into a quilt of fusty fabric
a torn tapestry of disaster.
I'm a rag doll of lumpy kapok
needled by insomnia
only the morning light
can tack me back together again.

Rose Docherty

Reflections on a dull day

I keep a diary, who knows why?
So many of my days are groundhog,
all the way from breakfast porridge
through to bedtime cocoa.
I shake up my routine, the pattern changes
but still the pieces stay the same.
My highs fall flat, my lows bounce back,
everything regresses to the mean.
And yet I live in interesting times.
I dig fresh garments from the wardrobe,
but still the mirror image looks like me.
I raid the supermarket aisles and recipes
to plan a change of diet. But I lack the casual
competence of every chatty TV cook,
it all turns into discontent and basic fuel.

Julie Anne Gilligan

RUMOURS

Listen to rumours, the world will end soon.
Hark at the gloom mongers, prophets of doom.

The threat is not minimal; it's a serious thing.
But let's put it in context: those alarm bells should ring.

How many toilet rolls can you fit in the cupboards
When the food's all gone like Old Mother Hubbard's

The black market's gone legal, profiteering in soap
But the hoarders are selfish now some have no hope

No pasta to be found, it all went in a trice
If you're lucky you'll manage a small pack of rice

They said shelves would be empty come Brexit day
It looks like they will be but not the same way

Lock down, stay home, shut up the shop
The airlines and railways are in for the chop

The surgery's packed, the factories close
Whatever you do, just cover your nose

Working at home keeps you far from the crowd
What many have wanted but were never allowed

When the crisis has passed as it will in its way
Those prophets will find us the *next* judgement day

Susan Jarvis Bryant

A Timeless Villanelle

Let time be still; preserve and freeze
the bliss of this delicious day;
this dreamy state of seamless ease

where skin drinks in the sun-soaked breeze
and saffron gilds the gloom of grey.
Let time be still; preserve and freeze

the zephyr's tease in leafy trees
and scents of hyacinths and hay.
This dreamy state of seamless ease,

it quells the swell and shifts the seas
of destiny to due delay.
Let time be still, preserve and freeze

the lift that brings me to my knees
in praise of Gaia's gifts…replay
this dreamy state of seamless ease.

Stop the clock's tick-tocking! Seize
tomorrow! Make it melt away!
Let time be still; preserve and freeze
this dreamy state of seamless ease.

Jim Lindop

The Church Road

Come with me, let's walk
the church road, pad like its ghosts
its dusk-smudged edges.

The church squats, toad-like,
on its hillock. Names garnish
its memorial,

name on name on name:
"*Mort Pour la France*", village lads
morts sans sépultures...

That ancient lime-tree's
sucked in uncomprehending
offerings and prayers

      ◆ ◆ ◆

Pipistrelles quiver,
sensing weight in the cooling air's
darkening texture

Gibaut's watering
his sweltered, stressed potager
and hears his own ghost.

She rebukes, cajoles,
giggles, sings, weeps, flirts, then slips
into memory.

A barn-owl haggles
with its own demons, hush-winged,
feather-light, deadly.

♦ ♦ ♦

Come with me, let's stroll
the church road, sing with its ghosts
as night-time hovers.

Tim Field

On the Rack

Thyme has run out,
the cinnamon's stuck,
the basil's faulty
and the seasoning a jerk.
The chives are talking,
liquorice gone fennel,
mint out of condition,
now the mustard won't cut.
It's not wise to use sage,
cloves full of holes,
the turmeric's malignant,
the mace gone to ground,
chillies lie crushed...,
the herbs are all mixed up
and with no garam masala,
it looks like a total disaster!

Jane Avery

It wasn't the hot-tub that killed her

It wasn't the hot-tub that killed her
though the chlorine was making her cry
It was invoices, debit notes
grabbing her by the throat
that caused the poor woman to die

It wasn't the hot-tub she drowned in
or the water that smothered her breath
but the customers whining
Why's IPT rising?
That caused such an untimely death

The hot-tub endeavoured to save her
Soothing bubbles just kept her afloat
Though they helped with her rhyming
her words and her timing
it all came too late
The burden so great, and so heavy
She gave up the ghost

Kewal Paigankar

Evening at Redlands

You were always late
Arriving at my country mansion
After dark, long after the others
With their cacophony of laughter
Their high-pitched voices rising above the night air.
The small talk; the names dropping
The music from the car stereos
Drowned out by the noise in the hallway
Greeting the guests outside the front door.

But this was a prologue, a preamble
An aperitif to your grand entrance
As you moved like some divine apparition
Shaking hands, dispensing wit and enlightenment
Nodding and acknowledging, emitting a radiance
That eclipsed the glitterati.
Even among the famous hacks and scribes,
The glamour models, the celluloid stars,
The politicians, the law custodians,
The powder merchants
And the tablet dealers;
Amidst the drinks, the smoke and the substances
The little white envelopes on tables
Newly packaged and available;
Your glasses never got steamed
Till the other guests had departed.

You'd then visit the bathroom
Time and again, each visit taking longer
Till I'd find you, crouching low over the basin
Your nose almost touching the enamel
Dollops of splashing over Armitage Shanks.
Your face would be pale, your glasses smudged
You'd try and sit up before collapsing on the floor
In pain, whimpering in a low, soft voice,
What beautiful tiles you have!

(John Lennon at Keith Richard's mansion circa 1969/70)

Mark Bones

Unsocial media

It was on St Valentine's Day
that they sat on opposite sides
of a costly restaurant table
adorned with every suggestive trim.
    They spoke to the friendly waitress
more than they did to each other…
        Occasionally, dutiful smiles played,
over faces that seemed to search
elsewhere for apps to ease the strain.
            Instinctively, they lifted their phones
in hopes of purchasing consolation,
from other lives which might restore
a sense of dreamt sophistication,
to their shared trend of drifting apart.

K. J. Barrett

A Bar at the Folies Bergère, Edouard Manet, Twenty Years Later

Older now,
The stoop slight,
Holding herself well,
She sits at her scratched sunlit table
Signing postcards.

Sometimes, for a few francs
She will pose for the lunchtime crowd;
Their blurred reflections imaged in the mirror,
The fresh fruit and roses
Posing on the bar.

The big brown child's eyes
Still haughty and proud,
Strike like a hammer against an anvil,
Still as fresh as young flowers,
Even though the night is showing.

Jacob Lund

Caravaggio

Whisper anything in prayer and you'll upset the carts
So that the bodies fall. The streets get light
In the violet of the limbs that twist
Inside this small boy's hoop;
This is not something he should see,
Not least because his father soon will disappear
Into the flame and the shadow.

Tripping along with Borromeo
Into the lazzaretto and staying at home,
He senses that the time for fruit and flowers is gone,
Just as when we see a young man collapsed at the roadside
For two paramediche to bag, for oil to splash in candles,
For the candles in the eyes in the morgue to glow
And the light to sputter in the cold spaces, closed
To the dead visitors;
No need to ask the sisters of Lazarus now,
No need to hear the whispering at this Resurrection.

24-hour security glimpses a rosary
Draped lazily upon a frame, in a gallery
Where money can never buy pity or terror,
Not least in the hands of the wheezing benefactors,
While that other hand, if you like,
Dextera Domini,
Finds itself, Michaelangelo Merisi, little man,
In polythene.
But then you have known this all along.

(Caravaggio's father, Fermo Merisi, is thought to have died from the plague while the artist was still a small boy.)

Nigel Kent

He could've been a hero of a Thomas Hardy novel

*Indifference to fate which, though it often makes a villain
of a man, is the basis of his sublimity when it does not.* TH

They say if you beat
a dog long enough
and hard enough
you'll find the wolf within.
Fate certainly raised
a stick above its head
and brought it down
on their dad's back
time and time again.
Yet when his mother died
before a year was out,
they say he cried no more
than any other child;
and when their mum berated
him for letting siblings
strip him of his legacy,
he didn't say a word;
and when she lost the girl
she'd longed for
and left the sting of grief
upon his cheek,
he slunk away unheard
to the silence of his shed;
and even when returning home
he found the car again
outside their house
and curtains closed,

he did not make a scene.
It wasn't until
they found his diary
and let loose
his muzzled thoughts
that they heard the snarl
uncurling from his throat.

Diane Schofield

Library Book Bookmarks

A photograph of a horse with pink hooves.
A cross-stitched name, Angela, on frayed fabric.
Page numbers circled in pencilled daisies,
a slow way to find your place, I think.
An earring, pierced through page two, I guess
the book must have been bad!
Corners bent into triangles,
A pink origami elephant with a purple eye.
A slice from the hem of a skirt, silky and turquoise,
How did that happen I wonder?
Safety pins threaded into a chain.
An unopened packet of condoms,
a Boots receipt for condoms in a different book!
Did those readers ever meet?
A flattened Christmas decoration
and a squashed felt fairy.
Half a birth certificate, why?
A cat collar with bell – fur caught on the edges.
A fried egg, dull and rubbery…words fail.
A string of tiny sparkly beads.
Pressed flowers, pale and translucent.
The shaft of a screwdriver…no handle.
The menu from a Chinese takeaway.
A piece of inner tube, a credit card
and an invitation to a garden party.
All those lives to be imagined.

Karen Macfarlane

Ardmair Bay dawn

At the southern fringe of her kingdom,
Ben Mhor Coigach holds court
at dawn. A stole of white cloud,
soft as ermine, is draped
round one sandstone shoulder.
The sun, her consort, joyfully crowns
her craggy brow with gold.
The sea, her lover, casts up
strings of living diamonds
sparkling at her feet. The diamonds dance
on the waves, chased
by two swooping terns,
bold thieves,
themselves eyed by a cutpurse skua.
The east wind, court jester, bounces in,
tugs and twists the ermine cloud,
twitching, frisking, fraying, until
it's gone
and the mountain stands
unclothed and free,
to bestow her blessing
on the day.

Kate Young

How to Recover the Child

Take the man who wears the shape of the wind
and unfold him. Remove the cardboard skin,
let it drop in moon-soaked puddle,
then leave to dry in alley-dust street.

Ease cracked fingers from neck of bottle
once discarded in green-mouthed bin,
un-drink the contents, a gush of liquor
back-spit in the glass and screw the lid tight.

Pocket his mobile, access contacts
listed in D for Dealers and hit delete,
stare as numbers quickstep into air
requests hitting back of throat like hash.

Smother glass shards on knuckled fist,
meld oak splinters back to veneer,
re-unite pen with palm, outpour rage
through words he found so hard to form.

Seek help for the boy grown wild as a cub,
abandoned to feed off a mother's despair
his mane a disguise, the pain of growing
apart from the world, distant as stars.

Re-wind time, pause, catch the father
un-walk the path, pass hydrangea blooms
grown from seeding, leaving his son
to search vacant rooms and eyes.

Unspool the Polaroid film expose, re-capture
the smile of a boy in grass, his hand in mine
guiding soft fingers to shoulders of willow
patiently waiting for ball to smack bat.

Recover the child, a whirlwind of freckles,
fresh as bubbles in lemonade-fizz,
toddler-legs chasing shadows on lawns,
his laughter wearing the shape of flight.

POETS

ACKNOWLEDGEMENTS

Karen Macfarlane's poem 'Ardmair Bay Dawn' was placed in the Scottish Mountain Writing and is published on the Mountaineering Scotland and Scottish Mountaineer Magazine
https://www.mountaineering.scot

www.ingramcontent.com/pod-product-compliance
Lightning Source LLC
Chambersburg PA
CBHW070457050426
42449CB00012B/3005